CHICKEN SOUP FOR THE SOUL®
CELEBRATES CATS

CHICKEN SOUP FOR THE SOUL® CELEBRATES CATS

and the People Who Love Them

A Collection in Words and Photographs by
Jack Canfield & Mark Victor Hansen
and
Sharon J. Wohlmuth

Health Communications, Inc.
Deerfield Beach, Florida

www.bcibooks.com
www.chickensoup.com

Subject matter, locality and/or people in the photographs may not be the actual locality or people in the stories. Names of certain individuals have been changed to protect their identity.

Library of Congress Cataloging-in-Publication Data

Canfield, Jack, 1944–

    Chicken soup for the soul celebrates cats and the people who love them : a collection in words and photographs by Jack Canfield & Mark Victor Hansen and Sharon J. Wohlmuth.

    p. cm.

    ISBN 0-7573-0148-7

    1. Cats—United States—Anecdotes.   2. Cat owners—United States—Anecdotes. I. Canfield, Jack. II. Hansen, Mark Victor.   III. Wohlmuth, Sharon J.

SF445.5.C34 2004
636.8—dc22

2004054332

Publisher: Health Communications, Inc.
          3201 S.W. 15th Street
          Deerfield Beach, FL 33442-8190

Cover design by Larissa Hise Henoch
Inside book design by Dawn Von Strolley Grove

CONTENTS

v

In ancient times cats were worshipped as gods. They have never forgotten this.

—Unknown

THE CAT WHO KNEW HOW TO LIVE

Cookie was a working cat. He lived in a New York grocery store that he kept mouse-free. Cookie was no slouch, and there wasn't a self-respecting mouse that would dare cross his path.

After patrolling the nooks and crannies of the store at night, he had the run of the neighborhood where he would spend his days wandering. As evening approached, you could almost set your watch by his return to the store. He would arrive promptly five minutes before the store closed.

One cool October evening, Cookie disappeared.

The store's owners and their children searched for him in vain.

The kids were brokenhearted. As autumn turned to winter, the snow began to fall, covering the streets. Everyone worried about Cookie, alone in the freezing weather. "How will he survive?" the kids asked.

Miracle of miracles, the following spring, Cookie magically reappeared, looking healthy and clean. Everyone figured Cookie must have been sowing his wild oats in another neighborhood.

Everything went back to normal at the store. Cookie once more checked all the nooks and crannies of the store to make certain there had been no unwelcome visitors while he was away. He did his job perfectly until autumn, when Cookie once again disappeared!

Once more there was considerable consternation by his owners and their children. *How would Cookie weather the winter snows and the freezing cold?*

The next spring, just when the baby leaves started to form on the trees, Cookie returned again!

Cookie's owners began asking neighbors for any information as to where he might have been. The kids asked their friends if any of them knew where Cookie went during the freezing winter months.

No one seemed to know.

Finally, one of the children rang the bell of an older couple who lived in a private house near the grocery store.

"You say, a big black cat?" the woman asked. "With white little paws? Oh, yes. My husband and I hated to see him out in the cold. So I gave him a saucer of warm milk. After that he hung around our house almost every day. But we were going to Florida for the winter, as we do every year. I felt so bad about leaving that poor little creature here with no one to take care of him in the freezing weather. So we bought a cat carrier and we've been taking him to Florida with us every year for the past two years. He seems to like it down there. Has loads of friends. But, between you and me, I think he prefers New York in the summer. I think he has a girlfriend up here."

Arnold Fine

ats don't belong to people.

They belong to places.

— Wright Morris

UNDER HIS SPELL

I can feel him watching me
Through golden eyes, unblinking,
And I can't help but wonder
Just what it is he's thinking.

I know his habits, I know his ways
But his moods are hard to tell
The only thing I know for sure is
He knows I'm under his spell.

For eating he's claimed my nicest dish
To nap, my favorite chair
And anytime I want to sit,
He's comfortably resting there.

For play, he's got expensive toys
To chase and romp and caper
But still he's only happy with
A balled-up piece of paper!

He's always begging for attention
To be scratched beneath his chin
And when my writing takes me away from him
He steals my writing pen!

Despite our unique relationship
People ask, "Just who owns who?"
It's really nice to have someone
To look forward to come home to.

And so, I stay enchanted with
This crazy pet of mine
For nothing keeps you spellbound
Like a furry, finicky feline!

Tami Sandlin

A kitten is chiefly remarkable for rushing about like mad at nothing whatsoever, and generally stopping before it gets there.

—Agnes Repplier

CONVERSION

Ihave always been a "dog person." As far back as I can remember, there were dogs in my house. Not cats, dogs. So when two coworkers found a tiny gray kitten eating out of the Dumpster near our office building and asked me to take him in, I agreed, reluctantly. "Only temporarily," I proclaimed, "I'm a dog person." My coworkers nodded their heads knowingly and handed me the warm little bundle.

The kitten was three months old when I brought him home. Weighing in at barely three pounds, he rode peacefully in the passenger seat, atop my gym bag, and waited patiently while I went into Wal-Mart, befuddled in front of the cat items trying to decide what to buy. I knew I would need cat litter and a pan, some cat food, maybe a toy or two. I made my purchases and returned to the car to find his small gray face with green eyes soften at the sight of me. Something inside me shifted a little bit.

Don't get attached, I told myself, *it's only temporary.*

I took him to the vet the next day, calling him John Doe. I announced loudly in the waiting room that I was in possession of a cat in need of a permanent home. Meanwhile, I tried not to notice the warm feeling I got as I felt John Doe purring in my arms.

Several months went by with no responses to my "Cat Needs Good Home" posters. Since he had started responding to my calls (as much as cats will respond), I officially named him Bonaparte. I thought it was a funny name and I wasn't keeping him anyway.

At some point during those months, Bonaparte started sleeping with me at night. He had a curious habit of laying down in such a way that his body always touched mine. When I shifted, he stood up, waited for me to get settled again, then lay down against me again.

I had never known cats could be so affectionate.

He performed the usual kitten antics that caused me to scream with frustration. He brought the curtains in my bedroom down so many times that I started telling friends that he was redecorating. His sudden bursts of energy that caused him to race frantically around the house in pursuit of invisible bugs left me shaking my head in amazement. He yowled every night by the front door to go out—until I got him neutered. He woke up at five every morning and parked himself on my chest; paws folded neatly under his body, staring at me intently until I finally woke up and drowsily stroked him.

Then there was the constant purring that never ceased to delight me.

When he was two years old and I had long since fallen in love with him, Bonaparte became deathly ill. He spent three months in and out of intensive care at the vet's office, and he required a feeding tube for most of that time. One night, when I had to take him to the emergency clinic, I slept by his cage because I didn't want him to wake up and not find me there. I took him to a specialist one hour from home, where he stayed for almost a month. I drove there every day to visit with him, cuddle him and brush him because he was so sick he had stopped grooming himself. The vets were grim about his prognosis. I remember standing in the hallway one morning, sobbing, begging them not to give up on him.

See, there were these cold nights that I had to get through without his warm body snuggled up against mine. The hole in my heart left by the loneliness was tremendous.

The vet finally determined that a risky surgery had to be attempted, although there were no guarantees for Bonaparte's survival. It was his last and only chance. Miraculously, Bonaparte came through, recovered and was able to come home a few weeks later.

Today he is six years old, and over the years I have brought home two other stray cats. Bonaparte worked his magic on them just like he worked it on me. They were unsure, insecure and frightened, yet practically melted in his presence. He grooms them, lays against them while they sleep, or touches noses with them as they pass in the hallway. His heart is so big that it spills out and touches the cold, hidden places in other hearts.

Somehow Bonaparte found that place in my heart. He found it before I even knew what was happening. And every night when he climbs into bed with me and arranges his body so that every part of him is touching me, I feel my heart fill with love all over again.

Kelly Stone

READER/CUSTOMER CARE SURVEY

CDA

We care about your opinions. Please take a moment to fill out this Reader Survey card and mail it back to us. As a special **"thank you"** we'll send you exciting news about interesting books and a valuable **Gift Certificate.** To fill out Reader Survey on line: http://survey.hcibooks.com.

Please PRINT using ALL CAPS

First Name _____ MI. _____ Last Name _____

Address _____ City _____

ST _____ Zip _____ Email: _____

(1) Phone # (____) _____ Fax # (____) _____ **Comments:**

(1) Gender:

_____Female _____Male

(2) Age:

_____ 12 or under	_____ 40-59
_____ 13-19	_____ 60+
_____ 20-39	

(3) What attracts you most to a book?

(Please rank 1-4 in order of preference.)

	1	2	3	4
3) Title	○	○	○	○
4) Cover Design	○	○	○	○
5) Author	○	○	○	○
6) Content	○	○	○	○

(7) Where do you usually buy books?

*Please fill in your top **TWO** choices.*

1) _____ Bookstore
2) _____ Religious Bookstore
3) _____ Online
4) _____ Book Club/Mail Order
5) _____ Price Club (Costco, Sam's Club, etc.)
6) _____ Retail Store (Target, Wal-Mart, etc.)

BUSINESS REPLY MAIL

FIRST-CLASS MAIL   PERMIT NO 45   DEERFIELD BEACH, FL

POSTAGE WILL BE PAID BY ADDRESSEE

CHICKEN SOUP FOR THE SOUL

CELEBRATES CATS

HEALTH COMMUNICATIONS, INC.

3201 SW 15TH STREET

DEERFIELD BEACH FL 33442-9875

JOY

Joy is
a cat's purr
that bursts forth
suddenly
and for no reason.
A rumble
amidst couch cushions
in late afternoon sunlight that
becomes rhythm.

Laura Cota

ats seem to go on the principle that it never does any harm to ask for what you want.

—Joseph Wood Krutch

ou can keep a dog; but it is the cat who keeps people, because cats find humans useful domestic animals.

—George Mikes

OPERATION "FELINE JUSTICE"

From the moment the cat carrier door swung open in our living room, Clyde the cat established his territory. He jumped out, hissing, and hopped up and down on the living room sofa. Certain that he had cowed the enemy into submission, he set out on his patrol through the house, establishing a watchtower atop the refrigerator and a safe house among the towels in the linen closet.

Clyde was the undisputed feline ruler for several years; he even grew a little soft, letting the human civilians pet his belly when he was sure no other animals could spy him. One day, another cat carrier arrived in the living room. Clyde was on a routine patrol of the perimeter when he spotted it. He circled around it, sniffing, and when he heard the tell-tale meow, he knew that times had changed. Operation "Feline Justice" must begin.

Clyde knew he couldn't proceed with a direct attack. The humans would send him scurrying from his adorable nemesis with a swat on the rear end. This wouldn't be dignified for the undisputed ruler of the house. But something had to be done, especially once the interloper had discovered his safe house and was found sleeping on the best towel in the linen closet.

The humans had a box that they put food into. They would push a few buttons, and minutes later the food emerged hot. Clyde spied on them from atop his perch on the refrigerator. He began to stand in front of the machine, pushing buttons with his paw to see what would happen. For days, nothing. Then, the door popped open and the light came on. Clyde walked in, pretended to sniff around, and, with the patience of a veteran soldier, waited. Soon the interloper hopped up on the counter and walked into the machine. And in a flash, Clyde was out. He pushed button after button, waiting for something to happen. Then . . . disaster. The humans.

"Why's the microwave open? Clyde, what are you doing? Bad cat! Don't play with that!"

Clyde ran to his former sanctuary, the linen closet, and waited until the coast was clear. He need only bide his time. There was another box, a box in which the humans put their clothes, and it had that interloper's name all over it.

Elizabeth Butler-Witter

Cat's motto: No matter what you've done wrong, always try to make it look like the dog did it.

—Unknown

KITTY COURT

There we were, the five of us, at home on a Saturday morning, puttering around our condo in typical weekend style: I in my idiosyncratic human fashion, a sequence of sitting, pacing, then sitting again; they in the forced acquiescence of domesticated, furred and feathered creatures. We share 1,000 square feet on the second floor, Mochi, Merlin, Kuzu, Rashi and I: two orange felines—one shorthaired, the other long—a cockatiel and a small but mighty parrot. The reality of natural enemies cohabitating in such a small space is certainly noisy at times, but much more peaceful than one would expect.

On this particular Saturday, our weekend routine was interrupted by the doorbell ringing. I opened the front door and was greeted by a woman in uniform. I think she was carrying a gun, but I can't be sure. She definitely had things dangling from a holster-like belt. Could have been a cell phone, maybe a walkie-talkie.

I greeted her with the mixed signals of a welcoming smile and a raised eyebrow. Slightly nervous, I uttered one of those classic "hellos" that ends on a higher note than it begins, more of a question than a real greeting. She identified herself as an officer of the county's animal control department. She asked if I had any pets. With no hesitation, I answered, "Yes." She then asked if they had their "necessary" rabies shots. I balked a little, hemming and hawing, and eventually said, "No." Then, unsolicited, I rambled on about my belief in a holistic lifestyle, how my cats were only fed special health food, that they never left the apartment, that I didn't go to doctors myself so why should they, except for an emergency of course. And the clincher: how my favorite cat, Scooter, died years before when I took her to the vet—on the way to the vet, no less! Surely, these were justifiable reasons for keeping my cats housebound and inoculation-free.

Steely-eyed, the stout woman with the long blond braid listened patiently to my story and when she finally found an opening to speak, simply said, "Well Ma'am, your cats have to have rabies shots. It's the law." I had thirty days to comply.

Not the answer I was hoping for. "Could I challenge the law," I asked, "by enrolling the support of a veterinarian?"

"You can try, but it is the law. Thirty days," she repeated.

We said little more. She wrote something up that looked like an oversized traffic ticket and off she went to knock on more doors. Apparently, my town had a sophisticated service of door-to-door animal control. Interesting. It would take a few months before I would regret opening the door.

A peculiar intrusion, I thought. It was so uncharacteristic of my routine that I simply went on with my day, with my life, and filed the experience in that part of my brain where, thanks to my age, information takes up no space by evaporating almost immediately. The visit was forgotten.

Six months later, I received two pieces of mail from the animal control department. Tearing open the first, I saw the name Merlin printed on the document and the word "citation" emblazoned across it, asserting that I owed the county more than $100 for neglecting to inoculate my cat. I ripped open the second envelope and there was another ticket citing Mochi for the same offense. In fine print, there was some verbiage about an option to appear in court. In all of my forty-seven years, I had only set foot in a courtroom once, and that had simply been for jury duty. I had been excused; so, short of mailing checks to civil attorneys to avoid traffic court, I had never participated in the county justice system.

What a shock. Thanks to me, Mochi and Merlin now bore the

mark of kitty criminals. After spending an entire morning researching my options, I decided to appeal my case in court, animal court, that is. But after many phone calls, I found that even veterinarians who labeled themselves "holistic" would not come to my aid.

I finally located a mobile veterinarian who would make a house call, saving my sixteen-year-old Merlin from a road trip to the vet and, in my mind, impending doom. Her pronouncement forced me to let up on my principles: Give Mochi a rabies shot (it's the law) and exempt Merlin because of his age. One hundred and fifty dollars later, I had proof of Mochi's fight against rabies and a waiver for the senior orange tabby cat to live the rest of his kitty life without shots.

I went to "kitty court," paperwork in hand, and found myself among what I considered to be very serious offenders. My cats and I were "pussycats," if you'll excuse the expression, compared to this lot: neglectors, abusers, owners of dogs that bit small children. *My appearance before the judge should be painless,* I surmised. In this room filled with true criminals, I was a conscientious objector, a model citizen, a model pet owner. My choice to avoid giving my boys shots was deliberate. I was the perfect candidate for a show on *Animal Planet.*

After I sat through eight other cases, they finally called my name and I approached the bench. To my left, in a lineup of officers I spotted the blond, braided one. As I approached the judge, so did she. Situating herself to my right, she nodded and smiled at me while a male officer stood to my left. Once the judge announced the reason for my appearance, I broke into the same oration previously heard by the officer to my right, about my strongly held beliefs and how I lost a cat on the way to the veterinarian. This time, I interspersed some smiles to my words and made an effort to project my persona of a loving and responsible "parent."

The verdict? I would have to pay half of the citation and commit to inoculating Mochi on an annual basis. *A small victory*, I thought. I backed away from the bench bowing like a Buddhist with a mouthful of "thank yous" and more nervous smiles. Next stop, the bailiff's desk to write a check and continue to express my gratitude.

A year went by and a small blue postcard reliably arrived in the mail to remind me of Mochi's impending shot. This time I didn't dawdle and called my trusty mobile vet to attend to the matter. The beginning of our now annual event, we chased Mochi down. His pupils turned into giant black saucers and his shedding fur tumbled around the room from fear. The doctor did her deed. We wouldn't see her for another year.

Now, if I were really disturbed, I could simply report that my cats were deceased and forgo ever dealing with the rabies police again. Bad karma to do that, I think. But, with my new mobile vet, a pardoned elder cat and a continued diet of health food, the five of us can continue our relatively peaceful life on the second floor. With a view of the treetops outside our back patio, it's a bit like a treehouse. No casualties between cats and birds to date. We are happy to report that not only are we rabies-free—we are happy here.

Kim G. Weiss

VAVOOM'S LESSON IN LOVE

The Bible says that "perfect love casts out fear." I had never seen that demonstrated until I met Vavoom, a tiny, feral, calico cat.

Vavoom blew in with a blizzard one winter, and spent her days with two male companions in the relative warmth and safety of the crawlspace under my house. Despite the temperatures dropping well below zero several times that January, Vavoom never showed any inclination to come into the house. I could *feed* her, but she insisted that I keep my distance, thank you very much! Like many feral cats, Vavoom and her friends viewed me as the enemy, a necessary evil that provided food and shelter, but one that could never be fully trusted.

Spring came, and Vavoom became pregnant. She remained in

the crawlspace of the house, popping out twice daily to meow at the back door for her dinner. She felt comfortable enough to ask for food, but would still flinch and run if I attempted to pet her.

Then the rain came. Lots of it. In one morning enough fell to turn my backyard into a small pond, which then began to drain into the crawlspace.

The power of the rain and wind had knocked over some potted plants I kept outside. I went out in the torrent to right them and noticed, running toward me, a very skinny Vavoom with something small and pink in her mouth.

With a look of urgency in her eyes, she came straight toward me. She dropped her parcel on my shoe and meowed.

It was a newborn kitten.

The kitten was hairless, premature, and turning blue from wet and exposure. I picked it up immediately and put it in the pouch of my sweat top to warm it. I picked up Vavoom without a struggle, and took them both into my utility room, where I had a cardboard box. I filled the box with soft rags, and placed the kitten in it. Vavoom jumped happily into the nest next to her little baby. I brought her a dish of food and some milk, sat down next to the box, and started to pet her. Instead of ducking away, Vavoom thrust her head into my hand and purred.

The next day, I found her other three kittens; they had drowned during the flooding. It seems Vavoom knew she could only save one, and believed I was her kitten's only hope of survival. Her desire to save her kitten's life was more important than her own fears and mistrust.

Vavoom and her kitten, George, are still part of my family. As a matter of fact, George is my brat cat—as friendly and companionable as his mother was shy and aloof. George has known only love during his life, beginning with the perfect mother's love that saved him.

Jean Fritz

ou will always be lucky if you know how to make friends with strange cats.

—Colonial proverb

MIRACLE FROM MULBERRY STREET

When I was very young, my family lived in an unremarkable town in Massachusetts on an unremarkable road called Mulberry Street. We had the only mulberry tree on Mulberry Street, and beside that was the house of a kindly old widow known to me as Mrs. Monahan.

Behind Mrs. Monahan's house was an enchanted garden. My sisters and I were not allowed to play there because it was full of exciting dangers: an old abandoned well which had never been capped and rotting garden sheds whose floor boards or roofs could collapse at any moment, trapping an unsuspecting explorer such as myself. For this reason, we were absolutely forbidden to cross into Mrs. Monahan's yard. The happiest moments of my life on Mulberry Street were spent in that garden.

It was an absolute forest as far as I was concerned, although my older sister said it was just a regular suburban yard with an overgrown garden. In my recollection, the trees were so thick and towering, they all but obliterated the sun, and I was sure I disappeared the moment I stepped into their shade. The barns were vast, ancient ruins ("Just a bunch of old sheds," my sister said) and sometimes when I crept inside, I could hear wild animals scurrying away. Wild roses grew through the walls—hints of past elegance. I never found the well, which, if I had, I'm sure would have been one of the old-fashioned stone types with a crank for lowering the bucket. ("Just a hole in the ground, and you're lucky you didn't fall in," my sister said. "I'm telling.")

No amount of scolding could keep me from that garden. I was certain it held secrets about the past, about Mrs. Monahan, about our neighborhood. At the very least, it contained magical animals that only existed in the wilderness. Then one day, my expectations were fulfilled.

My sisters were in school, but since I was still too young, I was left to my own devices for the whole glorious day. It was a damp spring morning and Mrs. Monahan's garden was carpeted with periwinkles. I heard a faint mewing from one of the barns and when I went in to investigate, I found a tiny white kitten huddling next to her mother and three other kittens. She was the only one alive, so thin I could see the outline of her tiny bones through her fuzzy kitten fur. I tried to pick her up, but she spat at me and ran away. I ran to get my mother, knowing her compassion for the starving kitten would outweigh her anger at my disobedience.

My mother quickly warmed some milk in a pan and I led her to the kitten. "You poor thing," she said when she saw the frightened, white shape. She looked as though she were about to cry.

We placed the bowl halfway between the kitten and ourselves and stepped away. The tiny creature ran to it and started drinking so fast we thought she would choke. She sneezed a few times, but drank all the milk. Another day or two, my mother said, and she would have died like the others. When the kitten was done gulping the milk, she curled up next to her dead mother and siblings and fell asleep.

After that, each time we put her bowl out, we left it a little closer to our house and slowly won her trust. We named her Miracle, because it had to have been a miracle that she survived, a miracle that I, who shouldn't even have been in the garden, found her.

By summer, she was letting us pet her a little, but she hissed if we tried to pick her up. Then it came time for our two-week vacation in Vermont, and we didn't know what to do with Miracle. We put our dog Lady and our other cat Minou in the kennel as usual and asked the neighbors to look out for Miracle and to feed her if they could.

The day we returned from vacation, Miracle met us as we pulled into the driveway. She started running from the woods of the garden to the car, but collapsed before she could make it. She tried a few more feeble steps, but then gave up and mewed faintly from where she had fallen. My mother was out of the car almost before my father could bring it to a complete stop. My mother was crying openly as she went to the starving kitten, but this time Miracle didn't resist. We brought her into the house and fed her some warm milk, stroking her ragged little body while she drank. After that, she became a regular house pet, just like Lady and Minou, affectionate and friendly. It was almost as if she had never been wild. Almost.

When I was eight years old, we moved to Vermont, where my mother had grown up. We bought a house in the woods—real woods where someone could get seriously lost. I spent all my free time outside, exploring a little farther from the house each day.

Two weeks after we moved, Miracle disappeared. My sisters and I thought wild animals might have eaten her, but my mother said not to worry. She told us that Miracle was trying to go back home to Massachusetts and that once she figured out she couldn't find her old home, she would come back to us. We were still fretting, so my mother told us this story.

"Back when our family was still in Canada, we were very poor. My grandfather decided to move the family some seventy miles away to try farming on better soil. At the time, they had an old dog named Méchant. Even though he was like a member of the family, grandfather thought it would be too hard for such an old dog to move, so he left Méchant with a neighboring farm family, who promised to take good care of him.

"A month or two after the move, the family received news that

Méchant had left the neighbors' house almost as soon as the family left. Grandfather knew the dog had gone out looking for them, but as he had never been to the new house, there was no way he could find them.

"One cold, Canadian winter night, the family heard a sound at the door. Your great-grandfather took out his gun in case there was a dangerous animal waiting for him outside, but instead he found Méchant, shivering in the cold. He was gaunt and wounded, his poor old paws encrusted with frozen blood. When Grandfather saw that dog, he got down on his knees, buried his face in Méchant's fur and cried like a baby. He vowed never to leave an animal behind again."

Every time my sisters and I would worry aloud about Miracle, my mother would remind us of that story. Sometimes all it took was for one of us to gaze wistfully out the window and sigh and she would tell us the story again. "If Grandfather's dog could find his way home to a place he'd never been before, Miracle can find her way back to us. Remember, she's still wild and has stronger instincts than most cats."

Seven months after we moved to Vermont, we heard a familiar mewing outside the door. We all looked at each other to make sure we weren't imagining it; Minou was curled up on the couch as usual. We all ran to open the door and there stood Miracle, skin and bones just like when I first found her. Her paws were bleeding and her fur was matted, but she started purring when she came in.

"See?" my mother said, with a twinkle in her eye. "What did I tell you?" But I could see she was just as thrilled and relieved as we were.

Miracle lived a long healthy life. She gave birth to many litters, and all grew into cats with personality and pride. It was a regal breed and as I sit here today, thirty-five years after I first found Miracle, one of her descendents, Chibougamau, sleeps curled up by my side.

Kim Chase

ime spent with cats is never wasted.

—Colette

THE CAT

I

In my mind she strides,
As though in her own home,
A beautiful cat, strong, sweet and charming
She meows so quietly, hardly to be heard,

So tender and distinct her tone;
Her voice, a purr or growl,
Is always rich and wise.
Therein lies her charm and her secret.

This voice,
Touches upon my darkest depths,

It fills me with lyrical verses
And delights me with its magic charm.

It softens the worst of pains,
It holds all happiness;
To say the longest phrases,
It has no need for words.

No, there is no music that can touch
My heart, that perfect instrument,
And make its most lively chord
Sing more vibrantly,

Than your voice, mysterious cat,
Angelic cat, mystifying cat,
In whom everything is as sweet and
Harmonious as an angel!

II

From her brown and golden fur
Arises a perfume so sweet, that
By caressing her only once, I am caught in its balm
All evening long.

She is the familiar spirit of this place;
She judges, presides, and inspires
All things in her empire;
Is she an enchantress? A goddess?

When my eyes are drawn like magnets
Towards this cat that I adore,
And she returns my gaze so gently,
I look into myself as well,

I see with amazement
The fire of her pale pupils,
Clear lights, living opals,
That contemplate me fixedly.

Charles Baudelaire

THE WINGS OF AN ANGEL

I watch as the beautiful warm sun shines down on his gentle young face. And the early summer breeze blows his long beautiful white hair. For a moment . . . it's as if I can see the wings of an angel, and then I blink and they're not there.

I watch as he walks with such style and grace, each step more graceful than the last. For a moment . . . it's as if I can see the wings of an angel, and then I blink and they're not there.

I watch as he plays with the innocence of a child. Pouncing on each wiggly toe or getting dizzy from running around in circles. For a moment . . . it's as if I can see the wings of an angel, and then I blink and they're not there.

I watch as he lies at the head of a sick child. His soft fur touches her itchy red skin and his musical purr becomes a sooth-ing lullaby. For a moment . . . it's as if I can see the wings of an angel, and then I blink and they're not there.

I watch as he looks out the window for each child to arrive home and brushes up against their legs as if to say "I've missed you," forgetting that the children are grown and have homes of their own. For a moment . . . it's as if I can see the wings of an angel, and then I blink and they're not there.

I watch as he lay on the lap of a tired old man, whose frail cal-lused hands gently stroke his pure white hair. And then they both sleep. For a moment . . . it's as if I can see the wings of an angel, and then I blink and they're not there.

I watch as the warm autumn sun shines down on his aging old face. And the crisp autumn breeze gently blows his beautiful white hair. For a moment . . . it's as if I can see the wings of an angel, and then I blink and they're not there.

Many years have passed since I last saw his face, but I will always remember how he walked with style and grace. How he soothed the pain of a child, or gave comfort by just lying around. For a moment . . . I close my eyes and I can see the beautiful, warm sun shine down on his angel-like face, and then I blink . . .

And I watch as he soars with style and grace! His long white hair gently blows in the wind. And his angel-like wings, they were always there! They simply were hidden in his beautiful white hair.

Joni Strohl

THE FOG

The fog comes
on little cat feet.
It sits looking
over harbor and city
on silent haunches
and then moves on.

Carl Sandburg

There are people who reshape the world by force or argument, but the cat just lies there, dozing; and the world quietly reshapes itself to suit his comfort and convenience.

—Allen and Ivy Dodd

OF DOGS AND CATS

My cat has decided he's a dog. The metamorphosis was so subtle, so gradual, I wasn't sure at first, but now there is no doubt. He's hanging up his feline boots and joining the ranks of the canines. He used to be quite content to be a cat; I am sure of it. And I have been racking my brain trying to figure out what I did to make him start his cross-species adventure. I can't come to any concrete conclusion. I have to admit it hurts a little. When we got him I was ecstatic to have a little kitten in the house. He was a sweet thing with big wide eyes and ferocious little meows. I am going to miss having the old him around. I can't shake the feeling it's because of something I did wrong. Surely I could have prevented this.

It started when the puppy came. Until that moment, the cat was blissfully unaware there was any other lifestyle for him to consider. I realize now perhaps I was wrong. Maybe he wasn't a particularly happy cat, and life for him has improved greatly since the puppy's arrival.

The bizarre part is, they hated one another at first. The cat would hiss his disgust when the poor little pup walked by, extending a claw and smacking the adorable creature squarely on the nose. I would catch them glaring at each other, the cat on the back of the couch, the dog on the floor below, barking in annoyance that the furry acrobat wouldn't cooperate with the rules of playful engagement. The cat would turn his nose up at the water dish; its bottom filled with sand brought in on the puppy's curious snout. I fretted over how we would function with such discord in the household. I had given up hope of the two of them ever finding common ground. I really have no idea when the shift of attitude occurred. I wish I had been paying closer attention.

To his credit, the cat tried to keep his transformation a secret. He would sneak into the dog's dish at night, devouring the crunchy food made especially for canines. He'd pick at his feline meal in the morning while I was watching. He struggled with his gluttonous cravings; and I feared he had developed an eating disorder.

He would sit by the window on the puppy's favorite chair and emit a low menacing growl when strangers approached, turning it into a half-baked meow when one of us would pass by. Often we would mistake the sound for an imminent fur ball and rush him to the laundry room to hack it up in peace. I understand now how wrong we were and how we should have faced the situation then. Our careless assumptions have led to a glimmer of resentment on his behalf. Hopefully that will heal in time.

There was the tail chasing when he believed we were asleep;

the bone grabbing while our backs were turned; the attempts at learning to pant while he was hidden under the kitchen table; the refusal to use the litter box, instead holding out for a more exciting, slightly exotic spot in the garden next to the dog's diggings; and the gleeful looks he tried to conceal as bath time approached. All the while I made excuses to ignore what was happening: a mistaken action; a blurred line of vision, a strange shift in light that made it seem like he was exhibiting odd behavior. Denial is a funny thing and its roots grab onto fear to change one's perception easily.

I made the decision to seek outside help. I believed if the right person talked to my precious feline, he would be restored to his proper state and I could live happily saying I had a normally functioning cat. I phoned the animal shrink. I had to set up an assessment appointment a month ahead of time.

In the weeks that followed I tried to make a point of limiting contact between cat and dog. I was positive that if my cat could only have time apart from the object of his infatuation—time exploring the neighborhood to meet others of his own kind—the puppy impersonation would diminish and he would realize it stemmed merely from a lack of education about his feline peers. I pushed the cat into the outside world he had been hidden from for so long and he meowed mournfully at the door to be allowed to return to the comfort and security of his family. I held steadfast in my conviction and soon saw him wandering about the local haunts the other alley cats frequented. He was cured. I felt purged, like an unsightly blemish had been cosmetically removed from sight. My cat was doing cat-like activities! An unfortunate phase in our family life had passed and everyone could get back to the business of belonging.

I felt comfortable letting the dog and cat visit with each other again, first with a guardian to keep the cat from reverting back to his old habits, then on their own when I became certain all was well. Peace, I believed, had been restored to my life and things were as they should be.

Then something happened to change my newfound comfort. I admitted defeat and realized he must be allowed to alter his "feline" life permanently when I awoke in the middle of the night last week and stumbled into the kitchen for a drink. There, in the chair they had fought over when the pup first arrived, were my two pets, cuddled beside one another, blissfully content in each other's company. At first I was shocked! I wanted to run over, grab the cat by the scruff of the neck and shame him for his blatant display of mutated behavior under my roof! *What would have happened*, I thought insanely, *if my son had awoken instead of me and witnessed this deviant scene?*

Then I paused and gazed at them with the soul-searching look one has in moments of personal reflection. The cat had his head on the puppy's back and his arm was curled around in a loving embrace. The pup's eyes fluttered and he sighed contently—secure, warm and satisfied. The bliss they had found together was peaceful and pure. It was good. I set aside my narrow-minded opinions that night and entered a new realm of acceptance. I loved both my pets and how they changed from the time they were infants shouldn't impact my perception of our relationship. I love them for who they are . . . not what they prefer. I firmly promised myself that night to throw away my preconceived notions on what's "acceptable" to the general masses and pursue recognition of individual needs. My pets changed my heart, my core belief in how I view the world and that makes them all that more dear to me.

Now, if I could just get them to quit ganging up on the mailman.

Heather M. White

ne must love a cat on its own terms.

—Paul Gray

CAN I GO HOME WITH YOU?

Our daughter, Brett, had wanted a pet for years. But my husband, Gary, and I just couldn't see fitting the demands of a pet into our busy schedules. So Brett settled for collecting mechanical stuffed dogs that walked and barked with the touch of a remote control. When the batteries drained and her puppy was "as dead as a doornail," she moved on to her stuffed cats, making them jump and meow.

Gary and I realized that Brett's pretend pets weren't satisfying her needs for real flesh and fur when she started collecting tiny ants from the sidewalk, naming each one of them. We got her a little ant farm. But the twisting and turning tunnels between two sheets of glass soon bored her. She started taking the ants out and letting them crawl on her hands and up her arms and, unfortunately, under the furniture. Her dad stepped on some. I stepped on some. Brett cried.

We decided it was time for a real pet. The three of us went to The Humane Society and fell in love with a tiny, skinny calico cat with a face only a mother could love.

At first, Jessie was extremely affectionate, but as the cat grew accustomed to her new home and ruling her domain, her disposition changed—she was much more interested in looking out the window at the lizards and in napping. Cuddling wasn't part of her repertoire. Jessie and Brett went their separate ways; and for Brett, this meant back to her stuffed animals.

About a year and an half after we'd adopted Jessie, Gary was at the pet store buying her food when his eyes fell upon a little black kitten with big yellow eyes and an impish look, meowing at him from inside a little kitty cage. He called me at the office and said he'd found the perfect cat for Brett. Even his name was perfect—Weasley, like Brett's favorite character from the Harry Potter books. I could tell from Gary's voice that he had already fallen for Weasley.

"Yes," I said, "have the pet store hold him for us, but don't say a word to Brett about it." I wanted the three of us to be there together when Weasley came into our lives.

That same afternoon, when Gary picked her up after school, Brett showed him some new books she had gotten from her latest book order. She smiled broadly when she showed him a book about helping a kitten find a home. On the cover was a beautiful little black kitten, his face tilted up, peering out at the reader with big yellow eyes. The title emblazoned across the top was *Can I Go Home with You?* My husband smiled to himself, thinking about Weasley waiting at the pet store.

When I arrived home from the office that evening, we told

Brett that we'd all go out shopping but first had to stop at the pet store for food for Jessie. When we walked into the store, a group of children were crowded around the kitten cages. Brett walked over to join them and immediately noticed Weasley. She asked the store owner if she could hold him and then nuzzled her face into the little black ball of fur.

A little girl asked her, "Is that your kitten?"

"No, but I wish it was," she answered and turning to me said, "Isn't he adorable, Mom? Wouldn't it be great if we could take him home with us?"

"Sure would," I replied.

"Daddy, isn't he the cutest? I'd love to take him home."

"Me too," Dad answered.

"You mean we can?"

"Yes, honey. Dad's already made arrangements to adopt Weasley. He's yours!"

The tears welled up in Brett's eyes. "Are you serious Mom? Dad?"

We nodded in unison. "Oh my gosh," she said, and with Weasley snuggled in her arms, she ran over to the little girl she'd been talking to before.

"He *is* mine. He's *m*y kitten!" she cried to her. The other kids and customers and store staff turned to look at the little girl with her own real kitty.

Now, years later, when Brett climbs into her bed at night, Weasley still jumps up and lies right at her side. Then Brett opens the book with the little black kitten with the yellow eyes on the cover. "Okay, Weasley," she'll say, "let me read you a bedtime story." His big yellow eyes look lovingly at her and begin to close slowly as she reads him the story of how a little cat found his home.

Pat Holdsworth

In order to keep a true perspective of one's importance, everyone should have a dog that will worship him and a cat that will ignore him.

—Dereke Bruce

CONTRIBUTORS

Elizabeth Butler-Witter takes care of her cats full time, and in her spare time is a mother, writer and lawyer.

Kimberly A. Chase is a mother, a writer and a teacher. She has taught every age from preschool to adults. Currently, she teaches French at the middle school level. She has published fiction, essays and poetry in many publications. She is currently seeking a publisher for her first novel.

Laura Cota received her bachelor of science from the University of Massachusetts at Amherst and is currently a student at the Ventura College of Law. She works as a social worker investigating allegations of elder abuse. Laura is an avid runner who enjoys athletics, traveling, friends and, of course, pets.

Arnold Fine is a senior features editor of *The Jewish Press*. His column "I Remember When" has been continually published in *The Jewish Press* for fifty-three years. He has been honored by the National Association for the Furtherance of Jewish Education and the Jewish Teachers Association of New York State. He is married and has three sons and six grandchildren.

Jean Fritz grew up in a suburb of Detroit, Michigan, and graduated with a degree in English from Alma College. After fifteen-plus years in prepress production, Ms. Fritz chose to pursue her first love: agriculture. She owns Kitty Vista Organics *http://clik.to/kittyvista*. Her primary cash crop is (of course) catnip.

Pat Holdsworth, her husband, Gary, and their daughter, Brett, share their south Florida home with their cats, Jessie and Weasley. They are involved with the local Humane Society's "Howls for Towels" program.

Tami Sandlin has been writing poetry and stories since 1986. She has had over twenty-five poems published in various magazines around the country, as well as a series of short stories. She is currently at work on a series of paranormal mystery novels. She has six cats who allow her to share their space. You can write her at *crueangel@webtv.net.*

Kelly L. Stone has published stories in *Chicken Soup for the Sister's Soul, Chicken Soup to Inspire the Body & Soul, Cup of Comfort for Inspiration* and other anthologies. Her first novel will be available in the summer of 2004. Visit her online at *www.kellylstone.com.* Bonaparte is alive and well and doing his job of filling Kelly's heart every day.

Joni Strohl writes poems from experiences in her life. She enjoys her family and pets. Joni is currently a guesthouse manager for a major corporation in Ohio.

Kim Weiss, book publicist by trade and former owner of a public relations firm in Boca Raton, Florida, is often seen with orange cat fur and traces of pet birds on her wardrobe. Occasionally she escapes her small zoo by singing in a studio or balancing on one foot in her yoga class. She resides in Deerfield Beach, Florida, and hails from New Jersey by way of Oregon.

Heather White's passion for writing spans ten years. When not hunched over the keyboard, she enjoys spending time with her husband and children. Her future plans include finishing a novel in progress.

PERMISSIONS

The Cat Who Knew How to Live. Reprinted by permission of Arnold Fine. ©2000 Arnold Fine.

Under His Spell. Reprinted by permission of Tami M. Sandlin. ©1997 Tami M. Sandlin.

Conversion. Reprinted by permission of Kelly Leigh Stone. ©2002 Kelly Leigh Stone.

Joy. Reprinted by permission of Laura Cota. ©2002 Laura Cota.

Operation "Feline Justice." Reprinted by permission of Elizabeth Butler-Witter. ©2004 Elizabeth Butler-Witter.

Kitty Court. Reprinted by permission of Kim G. Weiss. ©2004 Kim G. Weiss.

Vavoom. Reprinted by permission of Jean Ellen Fritz. ©2001 Jean Ellen Fritz.

Miracle from Mulberry Street. Reprinted by permission of Kimberly A. Chase. ©2003 Kimberly A. Chase.

The Wings of an Angel. Reprinted by permission of Joni E. Strohl. ©2001 Joni E. Strohl.

Of Dogs and Cats. Reprinted by permission of Heather Mary White. ©2000 Heather Mary White.

Can I Go Home with You? Reprinted by permission of Pat Holdsworth. ©2000 Pat Holdsworth.